Sports car racing, 1930s style, recreated at a meeting of the Vintage Sports Car Club at Silverstone.
James Crocker's LG 45R Lagonda leads Riseley's Aston Martin. The ....
requirements, as are crash helmets and goggles (

SPORTS
1910 -

Ian Dussek

Shire Publications Ltd

CONTENTS

Set in 9 point Times roman and printed in Great Britain by C. I. Thomas & Sons (Haverfordwest) Ltd, Press Buildings, Merlins Bridge, Haverfordwest, Dyfed.

Editorial Consultant: Michael E. Ware, Curator of the National Motor Museum, Beaulieu.

British Library Cataloguing in Publication Data available.

ACKNOWLEDGEMENTS
   The photographs and much assistance in the production of this album were kindly provided by the National Motor Museum, Beaulieu.

COVER: *A 1934 Bugatti Type 57 with two-door Ventoux coachwork. Despite the closed body, the 3.3 litre twin overhead camshaft engine, which was offered in supercharged or unsupercharged form, gave the Bugatti a truly sporting performance.*

BELOW: *This graceful two-seater Bugatti was one of 38 Type 55s built at Ettore Bugatti's factory at Molsheim in Alsace. With its supercharged 2.3 litre twin overhead camshaft engine mounted in a racing chassis, the Type 55 represents that most desirable of all sports cars, the Grand Prix racing car adapted for the road. It was capable of over 110 mph (176 km/h).*

The Speed Six 6½ litre Bentley, driven by Woolf Barnato and Sir Henry Birkin, which won at Le Mans in 1929. It weighed over 2 tonnes. Bentleys won this event in 1924, 1927, 1928, 1929 and 1930.

WHAT IS A SPORTS CAR?

There must be very few boys — and girls — who have not at some time dreamed of owning a sports car. The thrill of the open road, the surge of power and the wind whistling through one's hair as the speedometer passes a hundred miles an hour — of such stuff are dreams and adventure books made. In reality, there are a few drawbacks, such as rain and cold, but nonetheless a real sports car has its own magic.

It is easier to say what does not, rather than what does, constitute a sports car. Large headlamps, wire wheels, knock-on hubcaps, bonnet louvres and aero screens indicate nothing. A real sports car combines power, speed, roadholding and sometimes braking. The balance is critical and for this reason a little 750 cc Austin may be more truly a sports car than a massive 7 litre vehicle, capable of twice the Austin's speed but which wallows like a bathtub. Sports cars emanated mainly from two lines of design. The first, epitomised by Bugatti and Alfa Romeo, was the production of a roadgoing replica of a Grand Prix car which the driver could identify with the racing machine. The car was fitted with items necessary to allow it to be driven on the highway, such as registration plates, wings, lighting, silencing and the like. A full width windscreen and weather equipment were sometimes added. Many engines were supercharged, that is the mixture of petrol and air was fed into the engine under pressure, whereas the normally aspirated engine sucked its fuel mixture in through carburettors. The second concept was that of taking a production design and turning it, by attention to performance, handling and design, into a sports car; MG and Jaguar were classic cases. The competition successes of such

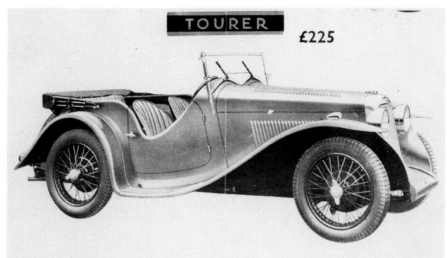

TOURER £225

Four seater, sliding bucket type seats in front with tilting backs giving easy access to rear seats. Special steering wheel and dashboard equipment includes large dial speedometer and large dial revolution counter. Triplex toughened safety glass windscreen. Folding hood with side curtains carried in rear squab. Chromium plated fittings. Pile carpet to tone with upholstery. Pockets to doors. Driving mirror. Dual screen-wipers. Tonneau cover with zip fastener. Spare wheel at rear. Full equipment including clock.

The 'technical specification' of this 1933 Hillman indicates that, despite its appearance, it was certainly not a sports car: more time should have been spent on the engine and roadholding and a little less on the bonnet louvres and revolution counter. As it was, the car was barely capable of 60 mph (97 km/h).

cars, which bore a close relationship to the model in the local showroom, provided a similar sense of identification.

Not all sports cars were identified with racing. Some, such as Sunbeam Talbot and Austin Healey, were associated with rallies, while others such as Morgan and HRG could be rallied, raced and trialled over a weekend and driven to the office on Monday morning.

Sports cars are still being made today but this album covers the traditional cars, built up to about 1960, with forward mounted engines and separate chassis as opposed to space frames. The dating is arbitrary but for practical purposes sports cars can be classified chronologically:

veteran and Edwardian to 1919
vintage 1919-1930
post-vintage thoroughbred 1931-1940
historic 1945-1960

There is no common factor about sports cars. Some, such as Bugatti, were individually built down to the last nut and bolt; others used many bought-in components. MGs were built in thousands while there were only seven Squires made. However, large or small, fast or not so fast, the true sports cars had character in pedigree, in handling and in individuality.

Only since the 1960s has the sports car cult extended past the eccentric group of beer-drinking, pipe-sucking enthusiasts who shared spares and information freely and traded their cars for a few pounds. The sports car makers little dreamed that in the 1980s hundreds of thousands of pounds would be paid for them at auction. Most would have been saddened; sports cars were built for driving, not to be put away as an investment or stuck motionless in a museum. Other designers would have smiled ruefully: many of the great sports car manufacturers ended up penniless and few ever made a profit.

ABOVE: *The 1937 3½ litre Speed Twenty Five Alvis was typical of its time. Despite carrying a heavy four-seater body, it was capable of over 95 mph (153 km/h). Alvis continued producing sports models up to 1967, although their principal business was in aero engine and military vehicle production.*

BELOW: *A competition sports car of the 1950s. This 1956 3 litre Maserati 300 S was based on the twin tube 250F Grand Prix chassis. The twin-cam six-cylinder engine was a modified version of the racing unit and the car had a maximum speed of around 155 mph (250 km/h).*

ABOVE: *The famous, but now discontinued, start of the Le Mans twenty-four hour race. Drivers ran across the track, jumped into their cars and the race was on. This is the 1950 event with Talbot, Delahaye, Delage and Bentley on the left and three XK 120 Jaguars in the middle of the line.*

BELOW: *A conventional grid start of a race at Goodwood in 1955. On the front row are three C Type Jaguars and a Cooper Bristol. Behind them are a Frazer Nash, an RGS Atlanta, a Jaguar XK120 and a BMW. Such line ups can still be seen at Historic Sports Car Club races.*

Racing on the public roads. This 1954 Mille Miglia picture shows Alberto Ascari with his Lancia D24 overtaking a Fiat on the Futa pass. As can clearly be seen spectator safety precautions were non-existent. Ascari won the race in just under 11½ hours at an average speed of 86.7 mph (139.6 km/h).

THE SPORTS CAR IN COMPETITION

Not every sports car is a competition model, but many made their names in a branch of motor sport.

Motor racing is almost as old as motoring. The early races were held on public roads and the tradition survived for some sixty years. Although the first true sports car race did not take place until after the First World War, several events became associated with sports cars.

The *Tourist Trophy*, first run in 1905 and held originally in the Isle of Man and later in Ireland, has taken many forms. During the 1920s and 1930s, for example, the event was run on a handicap basis so that cars as different as the 38/250 supercharged Mercedes Benz and the MG were on equal footing. Both of these cars won the event in different years.

Les Vingt Quatre Heures du Mans, 'Le Mans', is by far the best known. The race, run on a road circuit originally 10.7 miles (17.1 km) long, started at 4 pm and lasted for twenty-four hours under very stringent regulations controlling fuel consumption, repair work and other factors. There are several events running simultaneously within the race, but the car with the greatest distance covered at the end of twenty-four hours is regarded as the winner.

The *Mille Miglia,* the 'Thousand Miles', ran on public roads from Brescia to Rome and Bologna, then back to Brescia. Probably the most testing race of all and with hundreds of entries, it was discontinued in 1957 following fatalities.

The *Targa Florio* was held on a public road circuit in Sicily. In this and other sports car races held throughout the world, the cars were divided into classes according to engine size, often with extra

7

awards for team performances. There were many regulations governing the type, construction and driving of such cars.

In addition to these, almost every weekend there are lesser and club events for all grades of driver and types of sports car. These are just as competitive as the major events and the enthusiast can obtain great enjoyment from watching or competing in these meetings.

Rallies were run mostly on public roads, the object being to drive from one point to another maintaining a given average speed. This called for accurate map reading and a great deal of stamina. Penalties for arriving early or late at check points were the basis of obtaining a result. Rallies were at their most popular during the 1950s.

The *Monte Carlo Rally,* first held in 1911, was originally a sporting run in January to the warmth of Monte Carlo, but the event was later organised to enable drivers to start from places as far afield as Scotland, Sweden or Greece. After some four or five days driving, often in very difficult weather conditions, regularity and speed tests had to be completed, the driver and his crew having had a minimum of sleep.

The *Alpine Rally* is another long distance event, run with both day and night sections through the Alps and designed to test man and machine to the limit. Up to the 1950s, the roads were frequently primitive, but as the Alpine passes were surfaced the speeds and the demands on the cars and driver increased.

Many smaller rallies, notably those in Britain, relied for their success on very accurate map reading skill, timing and intelligence. These events were normally run at night and eventually their numbers and frequency made them a public nuisance. They are now very strictly controlled in Britain by the Royal Automobile Club, the governing body for all types of motor sport. Many major rallies are run now on closed forest roads.

The earliest trials were simply attempts to drive from one place to another. As the cars improved, steep hills were included and subsequently special hills, off the public highway, were added. These were not only steep but were frequently doctored with mud, rocks and water. Failure to climb these special sections resulted in lost points. The sport was particularly British and the premier events were the *Exeter,* the *Land's End* and the *Edinburgh Trials,* which each

A checkpoint on the 1956 London Rally. The marshal's car is a Sunbeam Alpine and competitors checking in include a Porsche 356 and an MG Magnette. The revolutionary layout of the Porsche was to have a profound effect on sports car design.

The Exeter Trial organised by the Motor Cycling Club is run in early January. Here a Morgan Plus Four claws its way up the lower slopes of Fingle Bridge. Low pressures in the rear tyres, the weight of the twin spare wheels and assistance from the passenger, or 'bouncer', all help to increase traction.

lasted approximately eighteen hours. In both trials and rallies, entries were not confined to sports cars, but attracted many of them. Trials were frequently run in limited areas, such as fields, with artificial hill sections marked out. Such events were very popular during the winter months.

Hill climbs, unlike trials, consist of an uphill section of paved road, such as a long drive. These may be several miles long in continental Europe, but in Britain are more often around half a mile (0.8 km), often with fast but short straights coupled with sharp — even hairpin — corners, the object being to drive the car

up as fast as possible. Over such a short distance the event is frequently decided by margins of one hundreth of a second. In such hill climbs the driver is driving against the clock and is alone on the course. Sprints were run similarly at such places as the promenade at Brighton, sections of race circuits such as Brooklands and other flat areas, frequently in a straight line without corners.

Today many of the older sports cars can be seen at rallies of a different type where interesting cars are brought together, frequently in aid of charity, and owners can meet and display their treasures.

ABOVE: *A paddock shot at Prescott Hill, Worcestershire, with examples of MG, Bentley and Alvis, together with many other interesting marques. Paddocks at such meetings are a magnet for enthusiasts and normally there are few restrictions on close examination of the cars.*

BELOW: *A social rally. This is a gathering of makes associated with the British Motor Corporation. (Left to right) a 1951 Morris Minor, a 1912 Morris Oxford, a 1905 Riley, a 1925 MG and a 1957 MGA.*

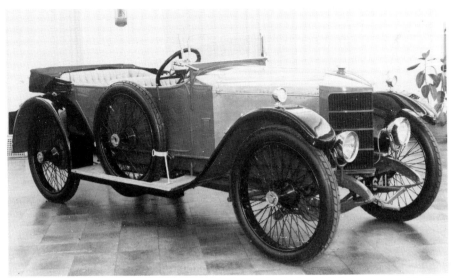

The 1911 Prince Henry Vauxhall can reasonably claim to be the first British sports car and its basic concept was perpetuated until 1928 in its later form, the Vauxhall 30/98.

ORIGINS

By 1900 motor racing had become established on public highways, frequently over long distances from city to city, such as Paris to Vienna. The cars driven by the early racing drivers were stark and simple, a light chassis with a nominal two-seater body and a large, heavy slow-revving engine capable of driving the car at speeds up to 100 mph (161 km/h). The second seat in the car was for the riding mechanic, whose tasks included pumping oil and maintaining air pressure in the petrol tank, changing tyres and carrying out running repairs.

In contrast, the wealthy motoring public purchased sophisticated versions for more sedate use. The bodies of such vehicles were built by coachbuilders. It was possible, for example, for a man to enter such a car without removing his top hat. These cars were designed to move quite slowly and although the requirement to have a man walking ahead of the car had disappeared in 1896, there was in Britain a general speed limit of 20 mph (32 km/h).

Between the extremes of the racing machine and the town carriage there developed the tourer, a machine capable of travelling long distances in a day, fitted with an open body, mudguards and weather equipment. Some manufacturers offered chassis supplied with two bodies, one closed and one open, which could be changed at will. The tourer would probably be driven by its owner rather than by a chauffeur. Touring was not for the faint-hearted; modern highway construction was in its infancy. Dust was an uncomfortable hazard in the summer and early attempts at surfacing the road with tars and patented processes were likely to add to the general discomfort. In wet weather mud and debris were a hazard to car and driver alike. Driving the early tourers was hard work: self starters were unknown, the acetylene lamps needed regular attention and the first screen wipers were hand-operated. Special motoring clothes were necessary: leather coats, gauntlets and goggles, with veils for the ladies. Supplies of petrol were infrequent and tyres were expensive and easily punctured.

11

A forerunner of the sports car, a 1901 four-cylinder Mercedes tourer. It is not difficult to imagine the discomforts of a long journey in such a vehicle and the huge mudguards indicate the degree of protection required from the primitive road surfaces.

As the car evolved, engine design became more refined, with more cylinders and shorter-stroke crankshafts. By 1910 competitive touring events such as that organised by Prince Henry of Prussia were established. From these the first true sports cars emerged, including the 5.7 litre Prince Henry Austro Daimler, designed and driven by Dr Ferdinand Porsche in the 1910 competition, and the 3 litre Prince Henry Vauxhall, designed by Laurence Pomeroy. The Vauxhall featured a light four-seater body with pointed radiator and was notable for its smooth top-gear performance. In 1913 the engine was increased to 4 litres and the resultant model, the 30/98, remained in production for fifteen years.

The French Coupe de l'Auto races also encouraged production of sporting models. In 1911 the event was for 3 litre cars and the winner was a Spanish Hispano Suiza Type 15T, designed by Marc Birkigt. The engine and gearbox were integral and production models were increased to 3.6 litres. Because the King of Spain had one the car rapidly became known as the Hispano Suiza Alfonso XIII.

There is little doubt of the racing parentage of this French Lorraine Dietrich, originally a 1912 Grand Prix car, but sporting primitive road equipment. Few early sports cars were fitted with front wheel braking.

12

Other manufacturers followed suit: Rolls Royce, Mercedes and Sunbeam (whose 12/16 owed much to their racing cars) produced models and the 100 horsepower Issota Fraschini used a massive 10.6 litre four-cylinder engine and weighed over 2 tonnes, twice as much as the Vauxhall.

At the other end of the scale, small cars such as the 1.3 litre Type 13 produced by Ettore Bugatti at Molsheim more than compensated in handling for what they gave away in brute force. Younger, less affluent enthusiasts used motorcycle components as the basis for light three- and four-wheeled vehicles. Initially these had crude frames and single-gear belt transmission, but they evolved into rapid cyclecars, of which the Morgan and the GN were best known.

This initial flowering of the sports car was short-lived since in August 1914 the First World War halted production. Sadly, many of the early cars became war casualties, but the development of technology in aeronautical engineering was to benefit engine design and production technology once peace returned in 1918.

A 1912 3.6 litre Hispano Suiza Alfonso XIII, now owned by Briggs Cunningham in the USA.

ABOVE: *The straight-eight engine of the 2.3 litre Type 35 Bugatti. The design is notable for a cleanliness and simplicity which has never been surpassed. The drive at the rear of the camshaft (top left) operates the magneto and the steering column and box is also visible (bottom left).*

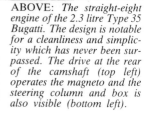

LEFT CENTRE: *The cockpit of a 4½ litre Bentley is an example of combined craftsmanship and practicality. A 4½ litre model finished first at Le Mans in 1928 but the later supercharged versions, of which W. O. Bentley disapproved, were unreliable competitively.*

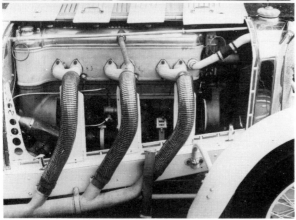

LEFT LOWER: *The engine of the 7 litre Mercedes Benz 38/250. The supercharger was mounted on the front and could be engaged as required by means of a clutch.*

Stripped of lamps and wings this is a classic Grand Prix racing car. This Type 35 Bugatti dates from 1925. The special alloy wheels are integral with the brake drums.

1919-1930

After the armistice in 1918 car manufacturers enthusiastically resumed production and for some three years cars of all shapes and sizes poured out of the factories. At the top end of the sporting scale, Vauxhall, Sunbeam and Hispano Suiza reappeared, the last named with a superb 6½ litre model. At the other end of the market thousands of inexpensive cyclecars, such as the GN, built by Archie Frazer-Nash and Ron Godfrey, used air-cooled engines and chain drives. GNs were also made in France under licence.

In the high performance field, Lionel Martin began building Aston Martins and other small capacity cars were produced by Alvis, AC and, later, Lagonda in England and Amilcar, BNC and Voisin in France.

The manufacturing explosion was halted in 1922-3 by an economic crisis and many marques disappeared. GN, for example, tried to build suburban saloons and Frazer-Nash went off to build cars under his own name. In 1921, W. O. Bentley, who had competed with DFPs before the war, produced the first of his own cars, an open 3 litre, with an engine design which drew considerably on established racing practice and also used aero-type aluminium pistons. Commercially the Bentley company moved from one financial crisis to another up to 1931, but during that time a series of 3, 4½, 6½ and 8 litre cars were produced which made the name Bentley synonymous with sports cars. Bentleys won Le Mans five times and even managed second place in the French Grand Prix against true racing cars. They attracted a group of wealthy drivers now enshrined in history as the Bentley Boys.

There were few cars that could take on the Bentleys at long distance racing but one which could was the 7 litre supercharged Mercedes Benz, particularly with Rudolph Carraciola at the wheel. The American Stutz also gave them a good run at Le Mans in 1929. The production Bentley had a speed in excess of 80 mph (129 km/h) but, in stripped trim, the car lapped Brooklands at 137.96 mph (222 km/h).

One of the reasons for the demise of many small car manufacturers was the

ABOVE: *Popular motor sport. A 750 cc Austin Ulster with a second Austin and an MG at Brooklands. These inexpensive cars could be purchased for less than £150 and could be tuned to produce speeds far in excess of their maker's catalogue claims.*

BELOW: *Cycle cars. The GN team before the start of the 200 mile race at Brooklands in 1922. The very light structure and air-cooled twin-cylinder engine can be seen. Brooklands in Surrey was the centre of British motor racing up to 1939.*

16

ABOVE: *The 1½ litre Alfa Romeo Type 6C evolved from the P2 racer designed by Jano. The larger-engined 1750 model was one of the finest sports racing cars of its day. Bodywork was by Zagato.*

BELOW: *The 1929 Lancia Di Lambda was notable among large Italian sports cars, with a four-seater body and substantial luggage capacity. While most manufacturers employed simple semi-elliptic front springs, the Lancia featured independent sliding pillar suspension.*

appearance in 1922 of the 750 cc Austin Seven. Initially the car had no sporting pretensions, but sports versions such as the Boyd Carpenter and Ulster models were soon offered. It was not long before another new firm, MG (Morris Garages), brought out the first Midget, the M, and the fight was on. The top speed of these tiny cars rose from around 60 mph (97 km/h) to over 100 mph (161 km/h) and they provided formidable competition in handicap events. Sold in large numbers at low cost, Austins and MGs became the first sports cars the general public could afford to own.

The continental sports car makers were very active; Lorraine Dietrich, Delage and Amilcar of France all supported competition, as did the Italians, who provided their sports racers with high quality tourers and saloons, such as those produced by OM and Lancia.

In 1924 Bugatti brought out his classic racing model, the Type 35. Although originally designed for Grand Prix racing, road-going versions were soon available with the supercharged 2.3 litre engine. A more practical version, the 1½ litre Type 37, was offered with the amateur sportsman in mind. The Type 37 engine formed the basis of the Type 40, a pleasant two- or four-seater road car. Bugatti's vintage sports classic was the Type 43, a model designed for all round performance in

long distance racing, rallies and hill climbs alike. The Type 43 had a top speed of 100 mph (161 km/h) compared with the Type 35 which could exceed 120 mph (193 km/h). Mention must also be made of Bugatti's masterpiece of the 1920s, the Type 41, a massive 12.7 litre, eight-cylinder motor, mounted in a 14 foot (4.3 m) wheelbase chassis. Just six of these magnificent tourers were built, regardless of expense; prices can be misleading, but the chassis was offered at double the price of the most expensive contemporary Rolls Royce.

Bugatti's main rival was Alfa Romeo. The P2 Grand Prix straight eight engine, designed by Vittorio Jano, was used as the basis of the 1½ litre 6C sports model. The capacity was raised in 1929 and the 1750 model was raced with considerable success. Other leading Italian manufacturers included OM, Diatto (notable as the first production of the Maserati brothers) and Lancia, whose Lambda model featured independent front suspension and a steel chassis which formed the body structure itself.

The 1920s abounded with exciting and unusual sports cars, Ballot, Tracta, Salmson and Chenard and Walcker to name a few. However, the basic instability of the industry was such that many disappeared in the international financial slump of 1929-30.

The short chassis 6.9 litre supercharged SSJ Duesenberg speedster built for the actor Clark Gable. Generally Americans preferred to buy European sports cars although Duesenberg, Cord, Stutz and Mercer all built attractive high performance models.

The 1931 1½ litre Aston Martin International model. This particular car was one of the works' team of that year. Aston Martin, under the direction of 'Bert' Bertelli, regularly fielded factory teams which, although notably successful at Le Mans (where they won the 1½ litre class five times), can have done little to improve the cash flow of the company. Over one hundred Internationals were built in two- and four-seater form.

1931-1940

The financial crisis following the Wall Street Crash of 1929 had a profound effect on sports car production. Almost overnight the demand for expensive playthings dried up. Bentley, for example, which faced bankruptcy, was acquired in 1931 by Rolls Royce, who proceeded to change the marque's competition image to that of a high speed, open, luxury tourer. The hallmark of the new Rolls Bentley was to be comfortable effortless driving, with softer suspension and lower ratio steering. Crash gearboxes, requiring skill and judgement to effect a clean gear change, were replaced by synchromesh. Weather equipment was improved but above all the weight of the cars increased, giving them sluggish performance despite their good looks.

During the 1930s many quasi-sports cars were produced, models with very poor performance but with wire wheels, aero screens and grilles over the headlamps. Most of these have long since rusted away.

Britain led the field in sports car production, the industry falling into two groups. At the less expensive end three major manufacturers, Austin with their range of 750 cc sports and later racing cars, Singer with their Le Mans models and MG were prominent. Of these, MG, with their overhead camshaft engines, were most successful, notably with the N and R series Midgets. These cars were manufactured 'in house' as were Riley, Alvis and Talbot among the larger cars. Riley's six-cylinder 1½ litre engine became the basis of the famous ERA racing cars. On the other hand many makers assembled a combination of components bought in from outside suppliers. For example, Henry Meadows Limited produced 1½, 3 and 4½ litre engines which powered Frazer Nash, Lagonda, HRG and Invicta cars and Moss gearboxes and ENV rear axles were found on a variety of different makes of car.

Despite the communality there was a wide range of cars from which to choose and a considerable opportunity for competition, from highly unofficial races

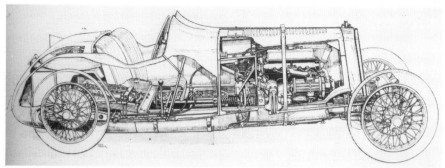

The 1932 Frazer Nash Nurburg model. Unusually, the supercharged 1½ litre engine drove the rear wheels via a set of chains instead of the conventional crown wheel and pinion. The suspension was comparatively rigid, giving excellent road holding and the two pairs of short, quarter elliptic road springs can be seen.

This 1937 4½ litre Bentley shows the change in company policy following the take-over by Rolls Royce. Coachwork for these cars was available from a number of sources, such as Vanden Plas, Park Ward and James Young.

The 746 cc MG C Type Midget, manufactured in 1931 and 1932, was a versatile performer and appeared in both supercharged and unsupercharged forms. A C Type won the 1931 Ulster TT and another won the Five Hundred Mile Race at Brooklands at an average speed of over 96 mph (155 km/h).

Mr. & Mrs. ......CLUTTERBUCK...................... Date ..13.../.Aug./..07

	Each	Total

Puppy of William Laurence

CHOCOLATE DAPPLE - Mother K.C. NO AE0373270
MINIATURE SMOOTH DACHSHUND.

9 WEEKS

(K.C. Pedigree Papers
- to follow)

TO PAY CASH
Vet checked - Vacinated - Wormed 13/8/07
H Stephanie Lawrence - 0 f
fine for; Penicillin. Halofuginone + SA626AV
to Formula above Dappers approx 1 week to 10 days.

£700·00

J.A.Laurence

from Oxford to the West End of London to regular meetings at Brooklands, Donington and Crystal Palace. There was a large following for trials and also rallies, which were social as well as competitive events. MG in particular supported all aspects of competition up to 1936, including record breaking.

From the mid 1930s there were further

changes. Riley joined the Nuffield group and MG switched to producing more mundane vehicles with their racing programme curtailed. Austin withdrew, as did Singer, leaving the private competitors plus Lagonda and Aston Martin (under a succession of owners and operating on a shoestring) to carry British competition hopes. Frazer Nash allied

RIGHT: *Trialling was very popular in the 1930s. Hills were suitably prepared to make them extremely difficult to climb and the occasional stream could catch out the unwary. The cheery driver of this 972 cc Singer 9 Le Mans is on the 1934 Brighton-Beer trial.*

BELOW: *In 1931 Donald Healey drove this 4½ litre six-cylinder Invicta to victory in the Monte Carlo Rally. Production of the Invicta ceased in 1934 although there were subsequent efforts to revive the marque.*

with BMW in 1936 to market Frazer Nash BMWs. The 328 semi-streamlined models, fitted with a 2 litre cross pushrod engine, proved a match for all but the fastest French sports racers.

Not that the traditional sports car was dead. Morgan, the pioneer of the three-wheel motorcycle-engined car, began selling four-wheelers in 1935, while H. R. Godfrey, who had collaborated with Frazer Nash on GN cyclecars up to 1922, produced the HRG, an uncompromising vintage-style model. Meanwhile William Lyons, who began by producing Swallow Sidecars and sports bodies for Austin Sevens, introduced his own SS cars, based on Standard parts. Initially these were merely stylish, but with the 2.6 litre SS 100 the forerunner of the low cost, high performance Jaguar had arrived.

In France, Bugatti continued the tradition of producing the ultimate in sports cars with minimal regard to cost. Over the decade, Ettore Bugatti moved from the racing machine-with-wings, such as the Type 35, towards the graceful and stylish Type 55 and 57 models. These largely reflect the styling ability of his son, Jean, but, unlike the Rolls Bentleys, they were still very much racing vehicles, what Bugatti called *pur-sang*. The Type 57, of which 710 were made in normal and supercharged versions, was the most popular and included the remarkable

ABOVE: *The T series MG Midget chassis, in this case a TA, with 1292 cc overhead valve engine. SU carburetters, manufactured by the Nuffield group, were standard. The chassis remained the basis of the T models up to 1954.*

BELOW: *The talented Swiss designer Georges Roesch was responsible for the 3 litre Talbot 105 which had a particularly fine record in the Alpine Rally and was also capable of lapping Brooklands at over 120 mph (193 km/h). This is the 1934 Alpine team, with drivers Mike Couper, Hugh Eaton and Tommy Wisdom. The Talbot company merged in 1935 to form Sunbeam Talbot.*

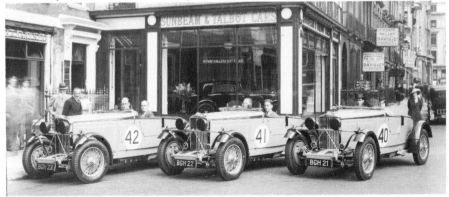

ABOVE: *The 1089 cc Imp was one of an attractive range of Riley Nines built between 1926 and 1935. The company also produced 1½ litre models and a series of stylish four-seater sports saloons.*

RIGHT: *The best known Frazer Nash BMW, the 2 litre 328 model, out-accelerates a Bugatti T55 from a Le Mans start at the Crystal Palace circuit.*

Atlantic coupés, influenced by aeroplane design.

Other leading French manufacturers, Delage, Delahaye and Talbot, all featured large reliable engines. As they had in the 1920s, Alfa Romeo dominated Italian sports car manufacture, with the 1750 and 2300 cc Monza models which were the major rivals to Bugatti. Later their Grand Prix racing engines were used in a limited number of coupés with all enveloping bodies. Mercedes Benz played little part in sports car activities, concentrating on luxury open cars and using the Grand Prix racing department for development work.

At the end of the decade W. O. Bentley joined Lagonda to produce the 4½ litre V12 engine for their Rapide models and for two advanced sports racers which made their debut at Le Mans in 1939. Later in that year, however, the Second World War put an end to motoring for over five years.

ABOVE: *Roadside repairs to the Chaboud/Tremoulet 3½ litre Delahaye during the 1938 Le Mans race. Despite various mechanical problems the Delahaye finished first at 82 mph (132 km/h). Passing is the Clark/Chambers HRG which finished second in its class.*

LEFT: *W. O. Bentley's last sports car design was the V12 4½ litre-engined prototype Lagonda, two of which raced at Le Mans in 1939, finishing third and fourth. Development was cut short by the outbreak of war.*

BELOW: *A 1938 Alfa Romeo 2900 B coupe. The engine was based on the Grand Prix P3 racer, with twin camshafts and twin superchargers. Unlike many 1930s cars the Alfa Romeo featured all independent suspension, while retaining a straight-cut crash gearbox. The competition version had a maximum speed in excess of 120 mph (193 km/h).*

The post-war Jaguar XK 120 which amazed and delighted enthusiasts used to the traditional lines of pre-war cars. This is the car made famous in international rallying by Ian Appleyard.

1945 - 1960

In 1945, because of post-war austerity programmes, there were few sports cars available in Europe. However, MG tapped a huge market in the USA by updating the pre-war T series Midget. Over 49,000 TCs, TDs and TFs were produced, mainly for export. The TC was not fast nor did it handle particularly well, but the 1250 cc engine could take tuning for competition both in its original form and also as the power unit for Lotus, Lester and Cooper.

Morgan and HRG continued much as before, but Frazer Nash and later AC made use of the 2 litre six-cylinder BMW cross pushrod head engine, now manufactured by Bristol. Donald Healey brought out his first Healeys. Historically these, along with Singer, Alvis and Lea Francis in Britain and Talbot and the very last Bugattis in France, represented the end of pre-war tradition and design. The whole concept of sports cars was changing. The first sports models produced by Enzo Ferrari in 1947 were fast and his 2 litre cars had much in common with the new Formula Two racing cars. However, Ferrari's day was to come.

The breakthrough came from William Lyons's Jaguar factory (which had dropped the prefix 'SS'). In 1948, a strikingly attractive two-seater, the XK 120, was introduced featuring a new six-cylinder 3.4 litre twin-cam engine, which was to power Jaguars for the next thirty years. Suitably tuned, the XK exceeded 130 mph (209 km/h) and was a winner in rallies and races, providing Stirling Moss with his first major competition success in the 1950 TT. It was a bestseller throughout the world and for the first time the public could buy a really fast sports car cheaply (£1,263). The XK 120 was followed by more luxurious versions, the 140 and 150, and by two competition models, the C (the first road car to use disc brakes) and D Types, which together won Le Mans outright five times in the 1950s. Despite their phenomenal performance, both were available to private owners.

Aston Martin, acquired by the tractor manufacturer David Brown, produced the DB series. The DB2 sports coupé proved particularly reliable and was followed by the DB3 and 3S, which showed considerable attention to aerodynamics, as did the 2 litre cars from Bristol, which, as an aeroplane company, had facilities for body design. Aston Martin's production models were essentially luxury sporting cars, but the later DBR racing sports cars brought them the world Sports Car Championship in 1959.

Ferrari achieved success less subtly. Deriving from Grand Prix experience, his big eight- and twelve-cylinder engines powered Ferraris to victory after victory. The 'Testa Rossa' series, driven by men of flamboyant character such as Gonzales, Hawthorn and De Portago, excelled in long distance racing. Production models featured the coachwork of Pinin Farina, Ghia and Michelotti but, unlike British cars, the Ferrari was beyond the mechanical ability of most enthusiasts.

Despite American interest, only one manufacturer, Cunningham, achieved an international reputation. Allard, Facel Vega and Healey used American engines, Sydney Allard winning the 1952 Monte Carlo Rally in one of his own cars.

In the early 1950s rallying ceased to be an amateur pursuit. Sunbeam Talbot developed the modern works team concept. Each rally stage was reconnoitred and practised while fuel, spares, service and tyres especially suited to the section were available. Within a few years the modern rally circus evolved, dominated by Austin Healey 3000s, which combined Austin 3 litre six-cylinder engines with

ABOVE: *The traditional lines of the popular MG TC endeared it to a generation of young Americans, to whom it sold in large numbers. Although undeniably a pretty car, it nonetheless gave many youngsters their first taste of competition.*

BELOW: *Some one hundred of these very fast Bristol-engined 2 litre Frazer Nash Le Mans replica models were built between 1949 and 1954. During the early 1950s a range of 2 litre models with all enveloping bodies was also marketed.*

The HRG, although vintage in concept, continued to be manufactured up to 1956, performing with distinction in all types of motor sport. The author's 1500 model clears a section on the 1962 Exeter trial.

chassis designed by the Healey concern.

The British Motor Corporation, formed by merging Austin and Nuffield interests, produced several best-selling models, the Austin Healey and also the MG T series replacements, the MGA and MGB. These catered for the mass market which flourished after the lifting of post-war production restrictions and as the result of aggressive marketing following competition victories.

Competition was provided by Standard-Triumph's TR2, introduced in 1954. Although their earlier Roadster was underpowered and overbodied, by drop-ping the 2 litre Standard Vanguard saloon engine into a sporting chassis they produced an attractive and competitive car. It was not perfect: roadholding was inferior to the power and it rusted, but so did MGs and Austin Healeys.

The European producers never managed to emulate the British. Mercedes returned to sports racing in 1952 with the 300SL, featuring overhead doors. Both the SL and the SLR, with its aerodynamic air brake, were successful, but their principal purpose was to boost sales of Daimler Benz products. In France, the impetus passed to the producers of small

Ferrari's early 2 litre cars were available in open and closed form. This is a 1950 Type 195 Berlinetta model. The previous year Luigi Chinetti drove a 2 litre to victory at Le Mans. Two weeks later he repeated the success in the Spa twenty-four hour race, despite turning the car over.

ABOVE: *The cockpit and engine compartment of the D type Jaguar. The famous XK twin-cam engine with its bank of horizontally mounted Weber carburetters can be clearly seen.*

BELOW: *Peter Clark at the wheel of an Aston Martin DB2 at Le Mans in 1952. With its 2.6 litre engine, the DB2 was never an overall race winner, but it followed Aston Martin tradition by being successful in its class, besides being a pleasant road car.*

specialist cars, notably Gordini, who used Simca components, and Deutch and Bonnet, who used Renault parts. In Italy many manufacturers relied on Fiat components, only Alfa Romeo and Lancia of the older marques remaining in major production. Maserati, no longer owned by the Maserati brothers (who now made OSCAs), brought out a few sports cars and some undistinguished production models. The competition Maseratis were notable for the 'birdcage', a body built up on an elaborate tubular framework.

This concept was developed further by British firms such as Lotus and Lola. Tubular space frames, replacing the chas-

28

sis and separate bodies, were built up around engines first by MG and Ford, then by Coventry Climax. Designed originally for fire pumps, the Climax motors proved world beaters from 750 cc to over 2 litres. Stressed alloy body panels provided additional structural strength.

These lightweight cars emanated in many cases from 'specials', combinations of proprietary parts assembled by enthusiasts such as Colin Chapman, Arthur Mallock and Eric Broadley. Their aim was to compete in motor sport cheaply and several makes were so successful that a demand for replicas was created. Before long Chapman was offering Lotus kits capable of being constructed at home and others followed, a considerable attraction being that the kit cars avoided new car taxes. Elva, Fairthorpe and Rochdale all had enthusiastic followings and designs became more sophisticated with the introduction of fibreglass body construction, which resolved the bugbear of much amateur construction, the curved body panel. Beneath the skin

ABOVE: *Bristol Cars Limited specialised in carefully streamlined bodies on their range of sports coupés. The 1953 2 litre 403 (left) shows refinements developed from the first production model, the 400 (right). In the 1960s the company switched to the 5 litre V8 Chrysler engine.*

BELOW: *This 1953 Ferrari chassis is unmistakably the result of competition experience. The engine is the Grand Prix 3 litre V12 unit with triple Weber carburetters.*

construction might be anything but conventional: for example, Marcos successfully employed a laminated wood structure. Most of the kit car constructors disappeared during the 1960s under financial pressure.

Another unlikely but important innovation occurred in the early 1950s. Before the war, Dr Porsche's rear engined racing Auto Union designs were reflected in his Volkswagen 'people's car', based on a four-cylinder air-cooled horizontally opposed engine. Using many Volkswagen parts and the rear engine concept, the Porsche established itself, first as a 1½ litre then in 1600 cc and 2 litre form. Its qualities of handling were outstanding and within a decade rear and mid engined sports cars were the norm.

These changes and, above all, the very high costs of research and development brought about the demise of many smal-

ABOVE: *The 1954 Sunbeam Alpine derived from the very successful Sunbeam Talbot 90 saloon. Critics dismissed it as a roadster and a cosmetic exercise, but nonetheless it was timed at 120 mph (193 km/h).*

BELOW: *The 2 litre Triumph TR2 was capable of 100 mph (161 km/h), sold very well and was the forerunner of a long series of similar models. It performed well in rallies and races but its accident record made it unpopular with insurance companies.*

Mercedes Benz sports cars were eye-catching and race winners. The 1952 300 SL featured gull wing roof-mounted doors, a difficult technical exercise. This is a 1954 production version offered as a very fast non-competition model, although luggage capacity was purely theoretical.

ler manufacturers. In Britain, Allard, Alta, Frazer Nash, HRG and others ceased production. Jaguar built one more traditional sports car, the E Type, effectively a road version of the D. However, the MGB, the marvellous Austin Healey Sprite/MG Midget and the conventional Lotus Elan represented the end of the line and twenty years later the traditional sports car was virtually extinct.

The Mercedes Benz 300 SL was superseded by the 300 SLR, a thoroughbred 3 litre racing car with open sports bodywork. Stirling Moss won the 1955 Mille Miglia with one but the success was soured when Levegh crashed his at Le Mans and over eighty spectators were killed. The experimental air brake at the rear is in the raised position.

FURTHER READING

Boddy, W. *Continental Sports Cars.* Foulis, 1951.
Boddy, W. *Vintage Motor Cars.* Shire Publications, 1985.
Conway, H. G. *Bugatti.* Haynes Publishing, 1963.
Georgano, G. N. *A History of Sports Cars.* Rainbird, 1979.
Grant, Gregor. *British Sports Cars.* Foulis, 1951.
McComb, F. Wilson. *The MG.* Shire Publications, 1985.
Montagu of Beaulieu, Lord. *Jaguar.* Cassell, 1961.
Posthumus, C. *The British Competition Car.* Batsford, 1959.
Wheatley, Richard C., and Morgan, Brian. *The Restoration of Vintage and Thorough-bred Cars.* Batsford, 1957.
   The monthly journals *Motor Sport, Classic and Sports Car* and *Thoroughbred and Classic Cars* regularly contain articles on sports cars. They also provide information on events and exhibitions at which the cars can be seen.

PLACES TO VISIT

Some notable museums and collections in Britain are listed below. Intending visitors are advised to find out times of opening before making a special journey.
British Motor Industry Heritage Trust, Heritage Collection, Syon Park, Brentford, Middlesex TW8 8JF. Telephone: 01-560 1378.
Doune Motor Museum, Carse of Cambus, Doune, Perthshire. Telephone: Doune (0786) 841203.
Midland Motor Museum, Stanmore Hall, Stourbridge Road, Bridgnorth, Shropshire. Telephone: Bridgnorth (074 62) 61761.
National Motor Museum, John Montagu Building, Beaulieu, Brockenhurst, Hampshire SO4 7ZN. Telephone: Beaulieu (0590) 612345.
Totnes Motor Museum, Totnes, Devon. Telephone: Dittisham (080 422) 357.

   The Vintage Sports Car Club runs a large number of rallies, trials, driving tests and race meetings. Two race meetings held at Silverstone Circuit, Northamptonshire, in April and July include some of the finest pre-1939 sports cars, both on the track and in the spectators' car parks. Races for post-1945 cars are frequently held at major race meetings throughout Britain. Details of these and many other sporting and social events can be found in the monthly diaries published in the motor sporting press.

The Wolseley Hornet was a borderline sports car. The 1271 cc Hornet Special, however, (far right) was capable of over 70 mph (113 km/h). This four car team was entered for a 100 mile (161 km) relay race at the Maroubra Speedway, Australia, in 1933.